LITTLE FLOWERS WITH BIG ATTITUDE

a science + art book
by Lori Adams

Little Flowers with Big Attitude
ISBN-13: 978-0-9895368-1-3
Library of Congress Control Number: 2013917425
© 2014 Lori Adams Photo

Published by Lori Adams Photo
Hopewell Junction, New York
www.loriadamsphoto.com

All rights reserved. No part of this publication may be reproduced or transmitted in any form or by any means, electronic or mechanical, including photocopy, digital, recording or any information storage or retrieval system, without permission in writing from the publisher.

Printed in the United States.

For the go-to ladies involved with this book: Eloise Adams, LuAnn Adams, Leah Adams, Karen Thompson and Bessina Posner Harrar. And for gardeners of all ages everywhere.

Plant Portraits

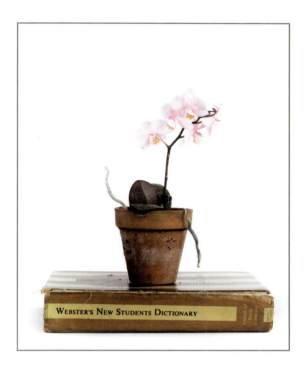

What's in a Name?

The common name (or nickname) for a plant can vary by region or culture. The scientific or binomial name is from the system developed by Carl Linnaeus in the 1700s that describes where a plant fits in with the rest of life in the universe. This name is in the worldwide language, Latin. The first part of the scientific name is the *genus* and the second part is the *species*. The genus is a noun and the species is an adjective. Sometimes the name is longer than two parts when a species has sub-groups called varieties, hybrids or cultivars.

The name can also be a starting point for your IMAGINATION...

Closely layered petals far
Opposite the roots,
Long stems with buds & blossoms on
Upright spreading shoots.
Multiple flowering
Beauties come somewhat late in spring.
Incredibly nuanced
Nature enriches
Everything.

There are over 50 species of this genus. The common name, columbine, comes from Latin for "dove." The formal name, *Aquilegia*, is from the Latin word for "eagle." This unusual variety, 'Nora Barlow', is named after the granddaughter of Charles Darwin. She studied genetics, gardened, raised six children and lived to be 104.

'Nora Barlow' Double Pink Columbine
(A. vulgaris var. stellata 'Nora Barlow')

Family: Ranunculaceae (Buttercup)
Genus: *Aquilegia*
Species: *vulgaris*
Plant height: 2–3 ft. (.6 to .9 m)
Approx. height of pictured portion: 5 in. (13 cm)

Scilla or Siberian Squill (S. siberica)

Family: Asparagaceae (Asparagus)
Genus: *Scilla*
Species: *siberica*
Plant height: 3–6 in. (7–15 cm)
Approx. height of pictured portion: 4 in. (10 cm)

Stretching in sunlight,
Classy, blue petals
Inch up.
Long, lithesome
Lovely leaves,
All softly sway in springtime breeze.

Scilla (pronouced with a silent *c*) is one of the earliest flowers to appear in the spring. It grows well under trees and naturalizes, or spreads, easily. It are usually blue, but also can be found in white, pink or purple. The leaves are basal, meaning they start at the base of the stem.

Leaves that shield
Independent stems,
Leaves with strength
Yet fluid.

OF THE

Vigorously
Aromatic,
Little white bells
Line up and up.
Eat not! Poisonous!
Yet visually alluring.

This little plant usually has two large leaves (and sometimes more), although just one is shown here in the larger photo. Small, orange-red berries form when the flowers are through blooming. All of the parts are very poisonous, which is a way the plant protects itself from animals and survives.

Lily of the Valley (C. majalis)
Family: Asparagaceae (Asparagus)
Genus: *Convallaria*
Species: *majalis*
Plant height: 6–12 in. (15–30 cm)
Approx. height of pictured portion: 6 in. (15 cm)

Tyrol Knapweed (C. nigrescens)

Family: Asteraceae or Compositae (Aster)
Genus: *Centaurea*
Species: *nigrescens*
Plant height: 24–36 in. (60–90 cm)
Approx. height of pictured portion: 5–6 in. (13–15 cm)

Knapweed is
Not a farmer's friend.
At times annoying. A
Purple-petaled
Weed with
Elongated leaves. Without
Enemies, they
Dominate the landscape.

A weed is any plant that spreads easily and becomes a nuisance. There are at least six species of knapweed that have taken over pastures and rangelands in the United States. Spotted knapweeds make a chemical that is poisonous to other plants and are disliked by most livestock. In some places, insects are used as bioagents to slow the plants' growth.

Gloriously globular with
Long, tall stems,
On to full
Bloom,
Emergent small gems.

Tantalizing, magnetic,
Hardy and strong,
Incredibly symmetrical,
Spherical throng.
Truly terrific in soft purple hues,
Leaves, grayish-green,
Enhance its virtues.

Although the small flowers are clustered into globular heads, the entire plant can grow up to 4 feet (1.2 m) tall.

Globe Thistle, pre-bloom (E. ritro)

Family: Asteraceae or Compositae (Aster)
Genus: *Echinops*
Species: *ritro*
Plant height: 3–4 feet (.9–1.2 m)
Approx. height of pictured portion: 2 in. (5 cm)

Gooseneck Loosestrife (L. clethroides)
Family: Primulaceae (Primrose)
Genus: *Lysimachia*
Species: *clethroides*
Plant height: 24–36 in. (60–90 cm)
Approx. height of pictured portion: 5 in. (13 cm)

Groups
Of
Ovals
Surround
Elaborate
Nexus,
Equally
Conjuring
Karma.

Little
Ones
Open
Sequentially
Ensuring
Splendid
Tapers.
Runners
Invade
Farflung
Environs.

Like geese at picnic grounds, this bushy plant can take over gardens. The spikes of flowers come from a large base and the curve of the stem forms a crook that changes shape as the small flowers bud, bloom and die from the bottom toward the tip of the cluster.

Open for business, bees!
Ready for the day.
Come and get it!
Hurry on down.
Incredible,
Delicious nectar awaits!

Flowering plants need help from insects to survive as a species. They must stand out while providing a benefit (nectar) that gets insects to visit and to keep coming back. One such insect is the colorful orchid bee. It can be a metallic green, blue, red, yellow or purple. It also has a very long tongue.

'Flora Ark' orchid (Sogo Gotris)

Family: Orchidaceae (Orchid)
Genus: *Phalaenopsis* × *Doritis*
Grex* name: *Doritaenopsis Sogo Gotris*
Plant height: 5–12 in. (13–30 cm)
Approx. height of pictured portion: 5 in. (13 cm)

Grex is used instead of *species* in the orchid family when species are bred by humans and the parents are from two different genera.

Chive (A. schoenoprasum)
Family: Amaryllidaceae (Amaryllis)
Genus: *Allium*
Species: *schoenoprasum*
Plant height: 12–24 in. (30–60 cm)
Approx. height of pictured portion: 4 in. (10 cm)

Alluringly aloft, lovely and soft.
Linear and long, tall and strong.
Leeks, garlic, onions, shallots and chives,
In gardens, in kitchens, enrich human lives.
Under the soil bulbous forms spread,
Marvelous benefits from tiptoe to head.

The *Allium* genus includes tasty vegetables with healthy benefits for humans, like the chives shown in the larger picture here. In addition to bulbs forming under the soil, there are also bulbils that form on top as seeds mature, like those shown in this garlic head.

Cluster of stamens with
Oval anthers create pollen grains.
Little leaves far
Under the flower are
Mighty rudders in the wind.
Bonnet-like blossoms
Inviting insects to
Nectar stashed in lanky spurs.
Enticing long tongues.

Stamens are the male flower parts that come forward from the center of the flower. Their ends are anthers, which make and hold pollen. The spurs are the portion of the flower trailing to the back that contain nectar. A nickname for this plant is "Granny's Bonnet" because it resembles a hat worn by an older generation. This variety of columbine is a hybrid, created by mixing seeds from specific parent plants.

'Swan Pink & Yellow' Columbine
(A. caerulea var. 'Swan Pink & Yellow')

Family: Ranunculaceae (Buttercup)
Genus: *Aquilegia*
Species: *caerulea*
Plant height: 12–24 in. (30–60 cm)
Approx. height of pictured portion: 4 in. (10 cm)

Pansy (V. × wittrockiana)

Family: Violaceae (Violet)
Genus: *Viola*
Species: The × means a hybrid or mix of more than one species.
Plant height: 6–8 in. (15–20 cm)
Approx. height of pictured portion: 6 in. (15 cm)

Poised, poignant faces
Adorn these precious jewels. With
Notable scent of ardor they
Symbolize "old schools."
Yesterday's craze, sweet bouquets.

The name *pansy* is from the French word *pensée* meaning "thought." Grown all over the world for centuries, this common flower has had surges of popularity and has been used to represent romance, nostalgia and lost love. *Pansy* also became the general name for a wide variety of *Viola* hybrids when botanists started mixing different species together in the 1830s. And even though *violet* (another common name for these flowers) is also the name for a color similar to purple, pansies come in other colors like red, yellow, orange and blue.

Hardy houseleeks,
Enchanting buds and blossoms.
Naturally
Sublime.

AN**D**

Clusters of crowns.
Headdresses hovering
In pale pastels above
Concentric colonies below.
Kinglike. Queenlike.
Simply succulent.

A succulent plant stores water in thick leaves. These flower stalks tower surprisingly higher than the main plant, which is very close to the soil. The name *hens and chicks* refers to a way this plant reproduces. Small offshoots (chicks) grow and stay close to the original larger plant (the hen). Succulent can also mean "tender," "juicy" and "highly interesting."

Hens and Chicks (S. *tectorum*)

Family: Crassulaceae (Stonecrop)
Genus: *Sempervivum* (houseleek)
Species: *tectorum*
Plant height (without flower stalks): 2 in. (5 cm)
Approx. height of pictured portion: 5 in. (13 cm)

Snowdrop (G. nivalis)

Family: Amaryllidaceae (Amaryllis)
Genus: *Galanthus*
Species: *nivalis*
Plant height: 6–8 in. (15–20 cm)
Approx. height of pictured portion: 6 in. (15 cm)

Svelte, sensuous, snowy white.
Nymph-like, nubile,
On stalks so right.
Withstanding winter and all its rough stuff.
Durable, yes! So sturdy and tough.
Resilient, robust, waxy-thick leaves give
Outstanding support: photosynthesis.
Puzzling specimen so out in the cold,
Segue to spring, this beauty so bold.

Galanthus is from the Greek words *gala* and *anthos*, meaning "milk" and "flower." *Nivalis* is from Latin, meaning "of the snow." The genus, *Galanthus*, has about 20 species. Two nicknames for *G. nivalis* are Fair Maids of February and Little Sister of the Snows. It starts flowering in late winter, often while there is still snow on the ground, and disappears underground by late spring.

High and
Over
Strong green leaves, buds are
Tall and
Arching.

The stalks of the hosta plant can be more than twice the height of the leafy mound below. This group of plants is known more for its foliage than its flowers. The subspecies and variations are generally called by the genus name, *Hosta*. There are over 1,000 varieties! It is an extremely popular plant among gardeners because of its wonderful leaf colors, textures and patterns and because it grows well in shade.

Plantain Lily (Hosta sp.)

Family: Asparagaceae (Asparagus)
Genus: *Hosta*
Species: *cathayana**
Plant height: 12–18 in. (30–45 cm)
Approx. length of pictured portion: 9 in. (23 cm)

*Because of the large variety of hosta species and cultivars and their many subtle differences, this is a best guess.

Bird's Foot Trefoil (L. corniculatus)

Family: Fabaceae (Legume)
Genus: *Lotus*
Species: *corniculatus*
Plant height: 12–18 in. (30–45 cm)
Approx. height of pictured portion: 7 in. (18 cm)

Blissful, bashful blossoms,
I
R
D'
S

Fetchingly, flowing freeform.
O
O
T

Totally twisted!
R
E
F
O
I
L

The plant family, Fabaceae, is also known as the bean, pea or legume family. It is the third-largest of the angiosperm families after the aster (daisy or sunflower) family and the orchid family. *Trefoil* means "three-leaved." The seed pod can look like a bird's claw. When it is widespread, this species has been used as food for cows and sometimes it is called "bacon and eggs."

Dear Daisy, my
Admiration abounds.
Innocence and
Simplicity describe
You.
    From your fluid
    Lines
    Emerge
    Abstract
    Bountiful blossoms. You are my
    Ambrosial,
    Nuanced,
    Everyday darling.

Daisy means "fine" and "first-rate." It was also a popular girl's name made famous in the song "Daisy Bell" (Bicycle Built for Two), a jaunty and funny love song written in the 1800s and still part of popular culture today. *Fleabane* means "harmful to fleas" and it was thought for a long time that this plant kept fleas away (which it does not).

Daisy Fleabane (E. annuus)

Family: Asteraceae or Compositae (Aster)
Genus: *Erigeron*
Species: *annuus*
Plant height: 2–3 feet (.6–.9m)
Approx. height of pictured portion: 9 in. (23 cm)

Purposeful Plant Parts

The flower is the sexual reproductive part of a plant that makes seeds. It has ovules (egg cells plus other cells) inside the ovary and has pollen in the anther sacs at the end of the stamen. Usually the flower needs pollen from other plants of the same species for the ovules to develop into seeds. The flower attracts insects, and sometimes even birds and bats, with colorful petals, attractive scents, sweet nectar and nutritious pollen. When insects like the bees shown here in the purple crocus and snowdrop come for nectar, they can get covered with pollen. They carry it to other plants they visit, while leaving some behind. After pollen lands on a stigma, it germinates, forming a tube that travels along the pistil to the ovules. After this fertilization, the ovules develop into seeds inside the ovary as it changes into the fruit. Fruits of different species can be soft and fleshy like blueberries, or hard like acorns and other nuts. Some fruits may contain pits like plums, or be encased by pods like peas.

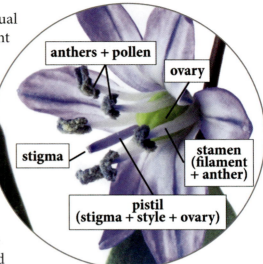

anthers + pollen
ovary
stigma
stamen (filament + anther)
pistil (stigma + style + ovary)

With sexual reproduction, the new plants contain genetic information from two parents. Wind, humans and other animals also play important roles in moving pollen between plants and moving seeds to new locations where a species may survive.

The stems or stalks are the support system of the plant.

They hold up the flowers and sometimes the leaves. They have tubes that move water and nutrients up from the roots and transport food from the leaves to other parts of the plant. There can be single stems or multiple stems from the same source; sometimes they start near the soil, and sometimes younger stems start at higher points along older stems.

The leaves are green because

they contain pigment called chlorophyll that captures energy from the sun. This energy, combined with carbon dioxide from the air and water and nutrients from the soil, creates glucose, the food for the whole plant. This process is called photosynthesis. Leaf size, shape and texture can differ incredibly from plant to plant. How the leaves are positioned on the stem also varies widely. Leaves may start at the base of the stem (basal), alternate in position from side to side, or start at the same point on opposite sides of the stem. When a plant has a cluster of flowers, like this daisy fleabane, the arrangement of the flower heads and the smaller stems on the main stalks is called inflorescence.

The roots of the plant act like filtering straws and soak up water and minerals from the soil. Little hairs come out of the roots and help the process. The roots also anchor the plant so that it doesn't fall over or blow away, and they keep the soil from being washed away by rain.

Stolons, rhizomes, bulbs and offsets

play important roles in a way that some plants reproduce, called vegetative reproduction. Stolons (sometimes called runners) are stems that grow horizontally away from a main plant along the ground.

They carry food and produce new shoots and roots that can develop into separate plants. Old runners dry out and new ones develop. Rhizomes are thick, tubular stems that also grow out horizontally from the main plant but are mainly underground.

They also store food and new plants grow from these structures. Irises and lilies of the valley have rhizomes.

Bulbs are storage systems that are swollen, fleshy layered growths on top of a short underground stem. The newer parts break off and develop into separate plants.

(A corm is similar to a bulb, but is a solid outgrowth from the base of the stem.) Tubers grow from rhizomes and stolons and are storage systems that help in growing new plants. An example of a tuber is a potato.

Offsets are small plants that grow above ground as part of the main plant. They start off as buds and develop into identical small plants that break off and form a new plant. Hens and chicks are examples of plants that reproduce this way. This kind of reproduction makes exact copies, or clones, of the parent plant.

Classification, Taxonomy and Phylogeny of Angiosperms (or Magnoliophyta)

Organizing knowledge of all flowering plants (angiosperms) in the world is a massive job. For over 250 years, the classification or taxonomic system has been based on the more outward parts of plants—shapes, characteristics and structure—using the Linnaean system of classification (named for Carl Linnaeus in the 1700s). But since 1998, the classification system for angiosperms began to change to reflect the ability to analyze DNA. Evaluating DNA is enabling botanical scientists to examine the phylogeny (study of how living things have evolved over time) of plants and this new method is revealing a wealth of genetic information. This system is called APG III, named for the Angiosperm Phylogeny Group that published its third report in 2009.

Species classifications and how they have been placed into genera (more than one genus) have pretty much stayed the same with the APG III system, but how these groups have been placed into larger groups (families, orders, superorders, clades, divisions, phyla and subkingdoms) of the plant kingdom has changed and is still changing. (One exception is some native plant genera that have changed much, including Latin names, to reflect new research.)

The charts on the next page show the difference in structure between the older Linnaean system of classification and the newer APG III system.

Linnaean System of Classification
Still in use for Animal Kingdom
example: Humans (H. sapiens)

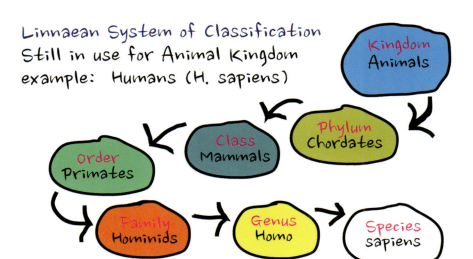

APG III System of Classification
Now in use for Plant Kingdom
example: 'Nora Barlow' Double Pink Columbine
(A. vulgaris var. stellata 'Nora Barlow')

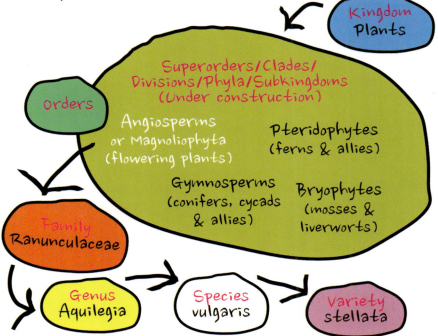

When there is human intervention

in breeding plants, new kinds of plants can be created. Making sure that pollen from one plant reaches a different plant consistently can result in a cultivar. The word *cultivar* is a combination of the words *cultivated* and *variety*.

Often plants are bred to bring out a specific characteristic like color, shape or size. Great effort has been put into creating many of the varieties of plants (like violas, columbines and orchids) that are seen at botanic gardens, garden centers and nurseries around the world.

If this is done with parent plants from the same species, then the new plant is called a "variety." If the parent plants are from different species of the same genus, then the resulting plant is called a "hybrid."

Further breeding of one hybrid plant with a different hybrid or another variety can result in yet another new variety. The format for naming these plants is defined in detail by the International Society for Horticultural Science.

Suggested Activities

Keep a science-and-art notebook and make a record of flowering plants in your yard or neighborhood. Lists, drawings and photographs are excellent ways to preserve information. You can also (with permission) collect, dry and save parts of the plants you observe. Write down when you saw them or collected them. Identify each with its common name and its two-part scientific (binomial) name as best you can.

Using your imagination and two of the plants you have identified, create your own cultivar keeping the parts of each you like the most. Draw your new plant. Give it a common name and its own binomial name based on the parents.

Author/Photographer Notes

All plant portraits in the preceding part of this book were from gardens or growing wild near the author in the Hudson River Valley. The exceptions are: the orchid from the New York Botanical Garden, Bronx, New York; the hens and chicks from Stonecrop Gardens in Cold Spring, New York; and the pansy from Sabellico Greenhouses & Florist, Hopewell Junction, New York.

Much inspiration for the larger photographs in this book came from botanical illustration, macro photography (exploring small things) and experimenting with studio lighting. The images in this book combine two kinds of photography that I enjoy—photography for science books for kids and fine art photography. Often the plant portraits are mistaken for paintings or watercolors, but they were all made in the camera under controlled, studio lighting conditions. There were only typical adjustments in the digital darkroom—contrast, dodging, burning and digital sensor dust removal.

The illustration similarities are in part due to 1) attention to composition, with precise placement of the plants, 2) often separate lighting for the plant specimens and for the background, 3) unusual depth of field achieved with high output studio lights and a small aperture and 4) the subtle colors possible with a large CCD sensor and quality lens.

Many more images can be seen at www.loriadamsphoto.com.

Other Books by the Author

Timeless Triops
Look, Ask and Learn About Butterflies
Triops - a very unusual creature

Photography example:
Narcissus set shot with gradated background

Resources and References

Art, Henry W. *A Garden of Wildflowers: 101 Native Species and How to Grow Them*. Pownal, Vermont: Storey Communications, Inc., 1986

The Plant List (2010). Version 1. Published on the Internet; http://www.theplantlist.org/ Accessed: 2013.

The Royal Horticultural Society Horticultural Database, available at http://www.rhs.org.uk.

Stevens, P. F. (2001 onwards). Angiosperm Phylogeny Website. Version 12, July 2012 [and more or less continuously updated since]. http://www.mobot.org/MOBOT/research/APweb/..

Acknowledgments

Botanical Consultants:
Henry W. Art, *Robert F. Rosenburg Professor of Biology and Environmental Studies at Williams College*
Michael Hagen, *Curator of the Native Plant Garden and the Rock Garden, The New York Botanical Garden*
Lynn Robbins, *Gardening Specialist*

Reader (ebook version): LuAnn Adams
Sound Editor (ebook version): The Sandbook Studio

Best efforts were made in plant identifications and scientific facts. Any mistakes in these areas are the sole responsibility of the author.

Thanks for reading.
Have a good night.
Ease into slumber.

Enjoy fancy and flight.
Name your own flower in
Dreams of delight.